This Sahara Media book belongs to:

....

Published in the United Kingdom by:

Sahara Media Ltd

The Gatehouse, 453 Cranbrook Road, Ilford, Essex, IG2 6EW

www.saharamedialtd.com

Content & illustration copyright @ Angela Dunkwu, 2017

All rights reserved. No portion of this book may be reproduced, stored in a retrieval system, or transmitted at any time or by any means, mechanical, electric, photocopying, recording, or otherwise without the prior written permission of the publisher.

The right of Angela Dunkwu to be identified as the author of this work and the owner of the illustrations has been asserted by her in accordance with the Copyright, Design and Patent Act 1988.

A CIP record of this book is available from the British Library

First printed in July 2017

ISBN 978-1-912329-00-7

Dedication

My baby brother, Patrick
I love him dearly
I pray he does well in life

Mum is having a baby

Written by
Angela Dunkwu

Illustrated by
M. Ali Çelik

My mum's tummy had started growing.
She ate a lot more food.

I didn't know why she always went
to the doctor.

I asked Dad if she was sick,
but he said no.

"Mum is having a baby!" he replied.
I was very surprised.

I started to try and do things myself.
Lots of it went wrong.

I tried to make myself breakfast,
but I spilled the milk.

I tried to bake a cake, but it got burnt.

Mum said that I didn't have to do everything, because I was too young.

The next day, I left my room untidy.
I did not clean my toys after
playing with them.

Mum told me off then, and I was
very confused.

I said to Mum, "You told me to stop trying to work so hard. When I did what you said, you told me off."

Mum replied, "What I meant was don't try and do too many chores. Do the work you are told to do.

Listening to my Mum, I tidied my room.
I put my toys back in the toy box.

Mum made pizza for dinner.
It was tasty.

We started talking about
different things.

I asked Mum if she was having
a boy or a girl.

She said she was having
a baby boy.

This got me thinking about what could happen when the baby is born.
All the boys in my classroom were very annoying.

I asked Mum and Dad if they could change the boy to a girl, but they said they couldn't.

I got really angry and stomped up to my bedroom.

My Dad tried to cheer me up,
but I ignored him.

That night, I had the worst dream ever.
I dreamt that my baby brother deafened
us with his crying, and that I had to
change his nappies.

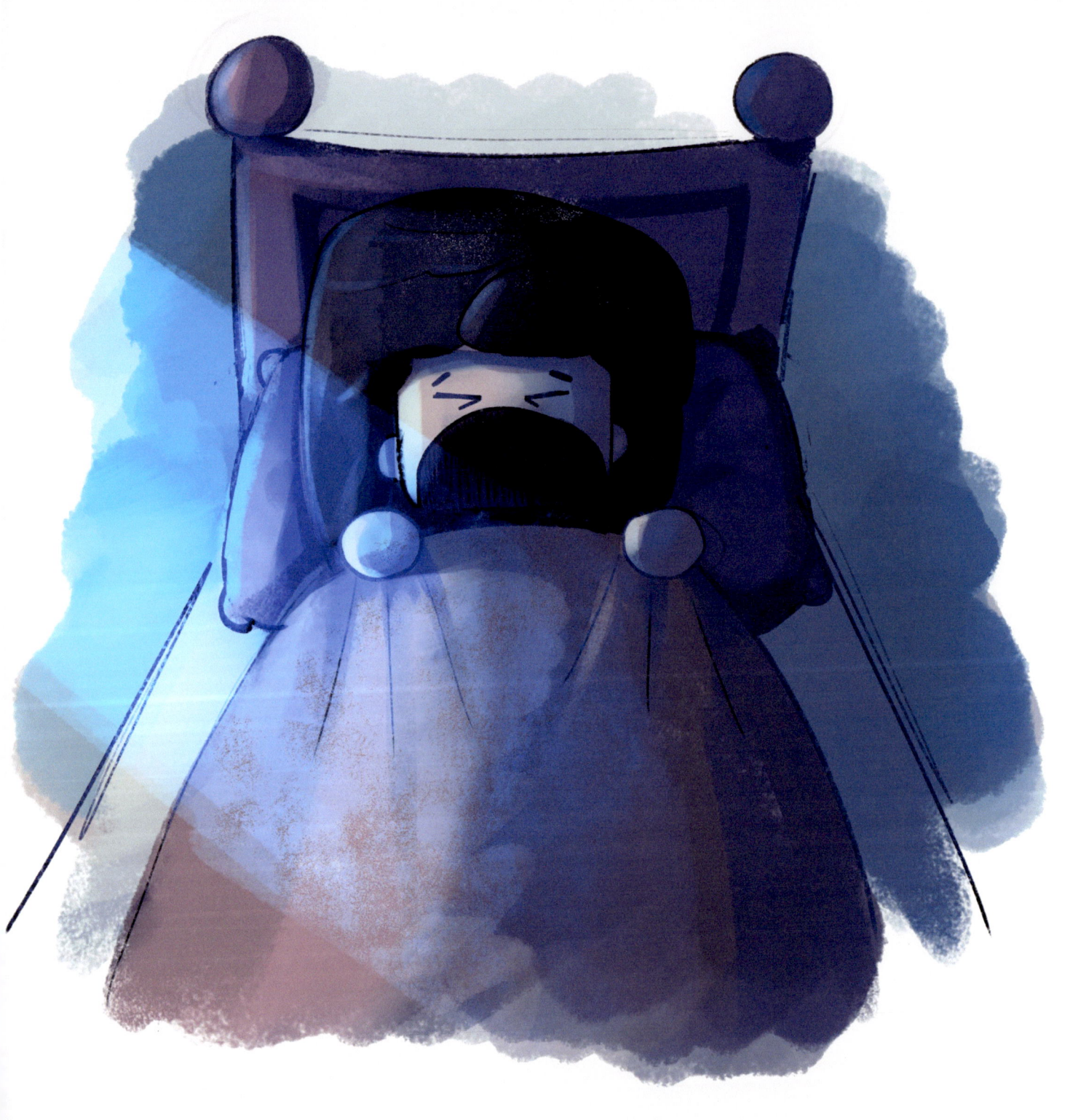

The bad dream made me
wake up screaming.
After a while, I heard Mum scream.

Dad came to my room and yelled, "Stop shouting. Your mum is going to have the baby!

He rushed Mum to the hospital.

She was in a lot of pain.

When Mum was having the baby,
I wasn't allowed inside the room.
I heard a lot of screaming
and shouting.

All of a sudden, I heard a baby cry. That was when I knew my baby brother was born.

When I was allowed in the room,
Mum was holding my baby brother.

Mum and Dad were thinking about baby names.
I came up with a perfect name:

Patrick!

Three days later, we took Mum and baby Patrick back home.

Printed by Libri Plureos GmbH in Hamburg, Germany